Y. A. TITTLE, FRANK GIFFORD, ALEX
WEBSTER, HOMER JONES, ER,
MARK BAVARO, ROOSEVELT BROWN,
JUMBO ELLIOTT, JACK STROUD, DARRELL
DESS, MEL HEIN, MICHAEL STRAHAN,
ANDY ROBUSTELLI, ROSEY GRIER, ARNOLD
WEINMEISTER, LAWRENCE TAYLOR, SAM
HUFF, HARRY CARSON, CARL LOCKHART,
MARK HAYNES, EMLEN **THE STORY OF THE**
TUNNELL, JIM PATTON, **NEW YORK GIANTS**
MATT BAHR, SEAN LANDETA, Y.A. TITTLE,
FRANK GIFFORD, ALEX WEBSTER, HOMER
JONES, DEL SHOFNER, MARK BAVARO,
ROOSEVELT BROWN, JUMBO ELLIOTT,
JACK STROUD, DARRELL DESS, MEL HEIN

THE STORY OF THE
NEW YORK
GIANTS

BY JIM WHITING

CREATIVE EDUCATION / CREATIVE PAPERBACKS

PUBLISHED BY CREATIVE EDUCATION AND CREATIVE PAPERBACKS
P.O. BOX 227, MANKATO, MINNESOTA 56002
CREATIVE EDUCATION AND CREATIVE PAPERBACKS ARE IMPRINTS OF THE
CREATIVE COMPANY
WWW.THECREATIVECOMPANY.US

DESIGN AND PRODUCTION BY BLUE DESIGN (WWW.BLUEDES.COM)
ART DIRECTION BY RITA MARSHALL
PRINTED IN CHINA

PHOTOGRAPHS BY AP IMAGES (ASSOCIATED PRESS), CORBIS (BETTMANN),
GETTY IMAGES (AGENCE FRANCE PRESSE, BETTMANN, PETER BROUILLET,
ROB CARR, FOCUS ON SPORT, STU FORSTER, LARRY FRENCH, TOM HAUCK,
KIDWILER COLLECTION/DIAMOND IMAGES, AL MESSERSCHMIDT, DONALD
MIRALLE, RALPH MORSE/TIME & LIFE PICTURES, NEW YORK DAILY NEWS
ARCHIVE, NFL PHOTOS, TOM PENNINGTON, AL PEREIRA/NEW YORK JETS,
ROBERT RIGER, GEORGE RINHART/CORBIS, JOE ROBBINS, JAMIE SABAU,
JAMIE SQUIRE, DAMIAN STROHMEYER/SI, ROB TRINGALI/SPORTSCHROME,
TIM WARNER/STRINGER)

NAMES: WHITING, JIM, AUTHOR.
TITLE: THE STORY OF THE NEW YORK GIANTS / JIM WHITING.
SERIES: NFL TODAY.
INCLUDES INDEX.
SUMMARY: THIS HIGH-INTEREST HISTORY OF THE NATIONAL FOOTBALL
LEAGUE'S NEW YORK GIANTS HIGHLIGHTS MEMORABLE GAMES, SUMMARIZES
SEASONAL TRIUMPHS AND DEFEATS, AND FEATURES STANDOUT PLAYERS SUCH
AS ELI MANNING.
IDENTIFIERS: LCCN 2018059137/ ISBN 978-1-64026-152-5 (HARDCOVER) / ISBN
978-1-62832-715-1 (PBK) / ISBN 978-1-64000-270-8 (EBOOK)
SUBJECTS: LCSH: NEW YORK GIANTS (FOOTBALL TEAM)—HISTORY—JUVENILE
LITERATURE. / NEW YORK GIANTS (FOOTBALL TEAM)—HISTORY.
CLASSIFICATION: LCC GV956.N4 W45 2019 / DDC 796.332/64097471—DC23

FIRST EDITION HC 9 8 7 6 5 4 3 2 1
FIRST EDITION PBK 9 8 7 6 5 4 3 2 1

COVER: ODELL BECKHAM JR.
PAGE 2: SAQUON BARKLEY
PAGES 6-7: VICTOR CRUZ

TABLE OF CONTENTS

GRIDIRON GREATS

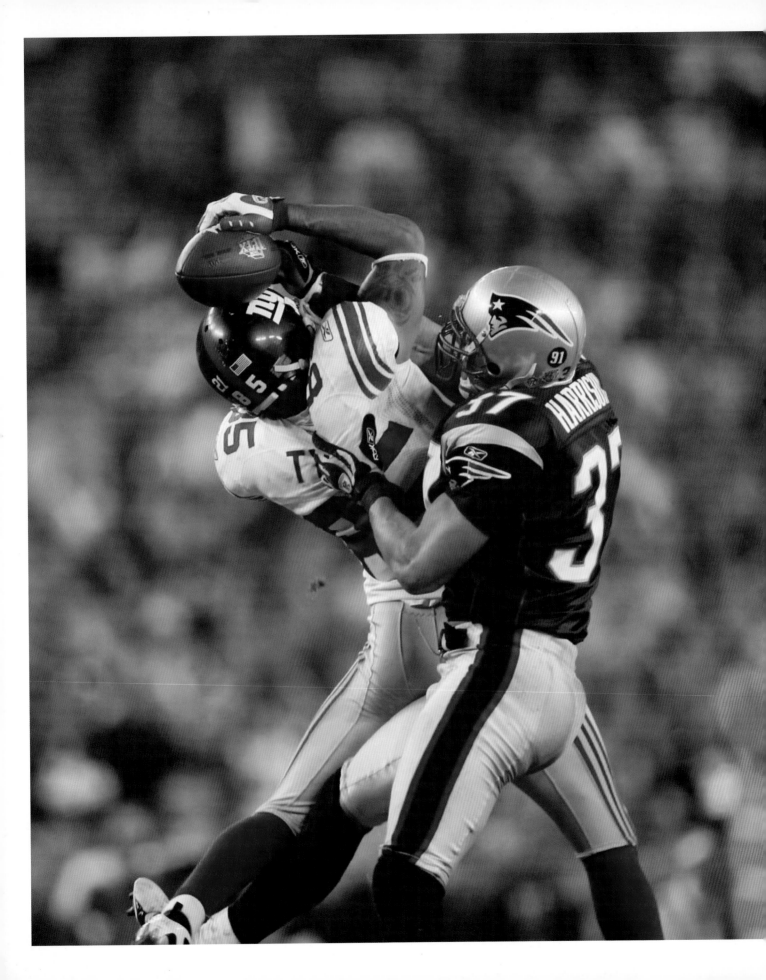

THE HELMET CATCH

Many people expected Super Bowl XLII to be a coronation. The New England Patriots were primed to go undefeated. Only one other National Football League (NFL) team had ever done that. Thirty-five years earlier, the Miami Dolphins had finished 17–0. Since then, the NFL had added two games to the season. If the Patriots won the Super Bowl, they would be the first team to go 19–0. Most experts predicted an easy win. The New York Giants had lost six games during the regular season. One loss came in the final game. It was against the Patriots.

NEW YORK GIANTS

ELI MANNING

In the Super Bowl, the Giants proved they were not pushovers. New York opened the game with a long drive. It marched 63 yards in nearly 10 minutes. But the Patriots forced the Giants to kick a field goal. New England took a 7–3 lead in the second quarter. The third quarter was scoreless. The Giants regained the lead early in the fourth quarter. Quarterback Eli Manning tossed a touchdown pass to wide receiver David Tyree. The Patriots surged back to a 14–10 lead with less than three minutes remaining.

Then, the Giants took over. They worked their way downfield. With only a minute left, a ferocious pass rush nearly sacked Manning. Somehow he escaped. He threw a long pass toward Tyree. The receiver jumped up. He got his hands on the ball. New England safety Rodney Harrison yanked him to the turf. Tyree pinned the ball

MEL HEIN
CENTER, LINEBACKER

GIANTS SEASONS: 1931–45
HEIGHT: 6-FOOT-2
WEIGHT: 225 POUNDS

GRIDIRON GREATS v
A CLOSE CALL

Mel Hein was an immovable blocker at center on offense. On defense, he was a devastating tackler. Hein nearly missed wearing Giants blue. After college, he wrote to several NFL teams offering his services. The Providence Steam Roller offered him $125 a game. Hein signed the contract and mailed it. The next day, the Giants offered $150. He telegraphed the Providence postmaster to stop delivery of the first contract. Although it violated postal regulations, the postmaster did as Hein asked. In 1938, Hein became the first offensive lineman in NFL history named Most Valuable Player (MVP).

PLAXICO BURRESS (NUMBER 17)

"WE SHOCKED THE WORLD, BUT NOT OURSELVES."

—ANTONIO PIERCE ON SUPER BOWL XLII

to his helmet. Officials confirmed the catch. Four plays later, Manning hit receiver Plaxico Burress with a 13-yard scoring strike. The Giants won, 17–14. It was one of the greatest upsets in Super Bowl history. "We shocked the world, but not ourselves," said linebacker Antonio Pierce.

The game will always be known for Tyree's unique catch. He was an unlikely hero. During the regular season, he caught just four passes. His Super Bowl highlight play earned several nicknames, including "The Miracle Catch," "The Reception that Ended Perfection." Perhaps the most enduring one, though, is "The Helmet Catch." Or, as Steve Sabol of NFL films called it, "the greatest play in Super Bowl history."

GRIDIRON GREATS v

ISTORY REPEATS ITSELF

The Giants faced the Chicago Bears in the 1934 NFL championship. It was a cold, icy day. The field was slippery. The Giants thought different shoes would give the players better traction. So their equipment manager borrowed basketball shoes from a nearby college. He returned at halftime. The Giants were trailing, 10–3. After the shoe change, they raced to a 30–13 victory. It was their second league title. In 1956, the teams matched up again in similar conditions. This time, the Giants wore sneakers for the entire game. They routed the Bears, 47–7.

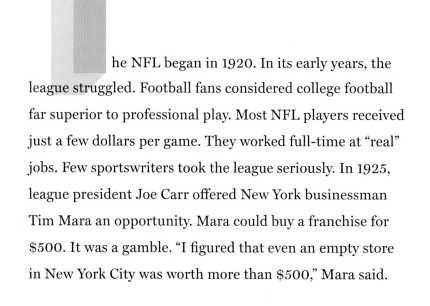

A SHAKY START

The NFL began in 1920. In its early years, the league struggled. Football fans considered college football far superior to professional play. Most NFL players received just a few dollars per game. They worked full-time at "real" jobs. Few sportswriters took the league seriously. In 1925, league president Joe Carr offered New York businessman Tim Mara an opportunity. Mara could buy a franchise for $500. It was a gamble. "I figured that even an empty store in New York City was worth more than $500," Mara said.

77

77 CAREER TOUCHDOWNS

136

136 GAMES PLAYED

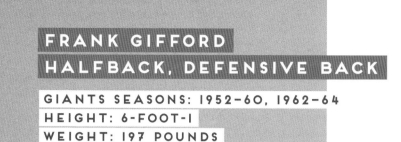

GRIDIRON GREATS v
MR. EVERYTHING

Frank Gifford had it all. He had good looks, strength, talent, and an outgoing personality. He could run, pass, and catch. He was a solid defensive back, too. He was chosen for eight Pro Bowls. "Frank was the body and soul of our team," said coach Jim Lee Howell. "He was the player we went to in the clutch." Gifford's best year was 1956. He was named the NFL's MVP. He led the Giants to their first title in 18 years. Following his football career, Gifford remained in the public spotlight. He became a television sports commentator and program host.

NEW YORK GIANTS

BENNY FRIEDMAN

The team played in the Polo Grounds. The field was already home to Major League Baseball's New York Giants. So Mara called his franchise the New York Football Giants. Mara and his two sons (ages 17 and 9) were the team's entire staff. To fill the stands, they gave away almost as many tickets as they sold. New York governor Al Smith was a friend of Mara's. He advised Mara, "This pro football will never amount to anything. Get rid of that team."

The Giants finished their first year with an 8–4 record. The most important game of the season was against the Chicago Bears. Chicago had signed star college running back Red Grange. It took advantage of his immense popularity. The team went on a 17-game nationwide tour. On December 6, the Bears played in New York. The Giants lost, 19–7. But 68,000 fans packed the stands at Polo Grounds. This included more than 100 sportswriters. Many people believe the publicity generated by that game saved pro football in the United States. Mara thought so, too. "My worries are over," he told a friend.

In 1927, the Giants won 11 games. Nine were shutouts. The mighty Giants allowed just 20 points to opponents. They won their first NFL championship. The following year, the team stumbled to 4–7–2. Mara wanted to sign star quarterback Benny Friedman. Friedman was regarded

TIM MARA

"BENNY REVOLUTIONIZED FOOTBALL. HE FORCED THE DEFENSES OUT OF THE DARK AGES."

—GEORGE HALAS

as the NFL's first great passer. In 1928, he led the league in both passing touchdowns and rushing touchdowns. It was the first—and only—time that feat has been accomplished. "Benny revolutionized football," said Bears owner George Halas. "He forced the defenses out of the dark ages." To get Friedman, Mara had to buy the entire Detroit Wolverines team. He paid $3,500.

Friedman worked similar magic for New York in 1929. He threw 20 touchdown passes. The Giants shot to 13–1–1. Their only loss was to the undefeated Green Bay Packers. New York took second in the league. The team came in second again the following year.

THE GREATEST GAME—
AND BEYOND

CHARLIE CONERLY

Throughout the next decade, the Giants remained fairly strong. The team featured players such as center Mel Hein and two-way back Tuffy Leemans. It captured nine division titles between 1933 and 1946. The Giants also won NFL championships in 1934 and 1938. In 1947 and 1948, they posted back-to-back losing seasons for the first time. The team returned to its winning ways in the early 1950s. The Giants' 1956 roster had a solid group of players. Offensive standouts included quarterback Charlie Conerly, running back Frank Gifford, halfback Alex Webster, and tackle Roosevelt Brown. Defensive end Andy

LAWRENCE TAYLOR
LINEBACKER

GIANTS SEASONS: 1981–93
HEIGHT: 6-FOOT-3
WEIGHT: 237 POUNDS

GRIDIRON GREATS ˅

"IT'S A BIRD, IT'S A PLANE, IT'S . . . L.T.!"

No defensive player disrupted an opponent's offense like Lawrence Taylor. "L. T." was always ready to charge the quarterback or take on a receiver. He made offensive linemen move too early. Quarterbacks fidgeted nervously. They dropped back sooner than usual, hoping to avoid a sack. Sometimes, opposing teams sent three players to block him. But even then, Taylor found a way to break up the play. "If there was ever a Superman in the NFL, I think he wore number 56 for the Giants," said former Washington Redskins quarterback Joe Theismann. L. T. was selected for the Pro Bowl 10 times. He was named the league's MVP in 1986.

132.5

132.5 CAREER SACKS

184

184 GAMES PLAYED

Robustelli anchored the defense. The Giants crushed the Bears, 47–7, in the 1956 NFL Championship Game.

Two years later, New York battled the Baltimore Colts for the championship. Today, the contest is known as the "Greatest Game Ever Played." The Colts tied the game late in the fourth quarter. It was the first time a championship game went into overtime. The Colts eked out a 23–17 win. After that, professional football was the country's most popular televised sport. "From that game forward, our fan base grew and grew," said commissioner Pete Rozelle. "We owe both franchises a huge debt."

In 1961, 35-year-old quarterback Y. A. Tittle joined the team. The "old man" led the Giants to three straight East Division titles. Each time, New York came up short in the championship game. After that, the Giants fell apart. They won just two games in 1964. Two years later, they posted a record of 1-12-1. Throughout the rest of the 1960s and '70s, the Giants had just two winning seasons. The offense could not score enough points to offset the porous defense. The team shuffled through coaches and quarterbacks. It

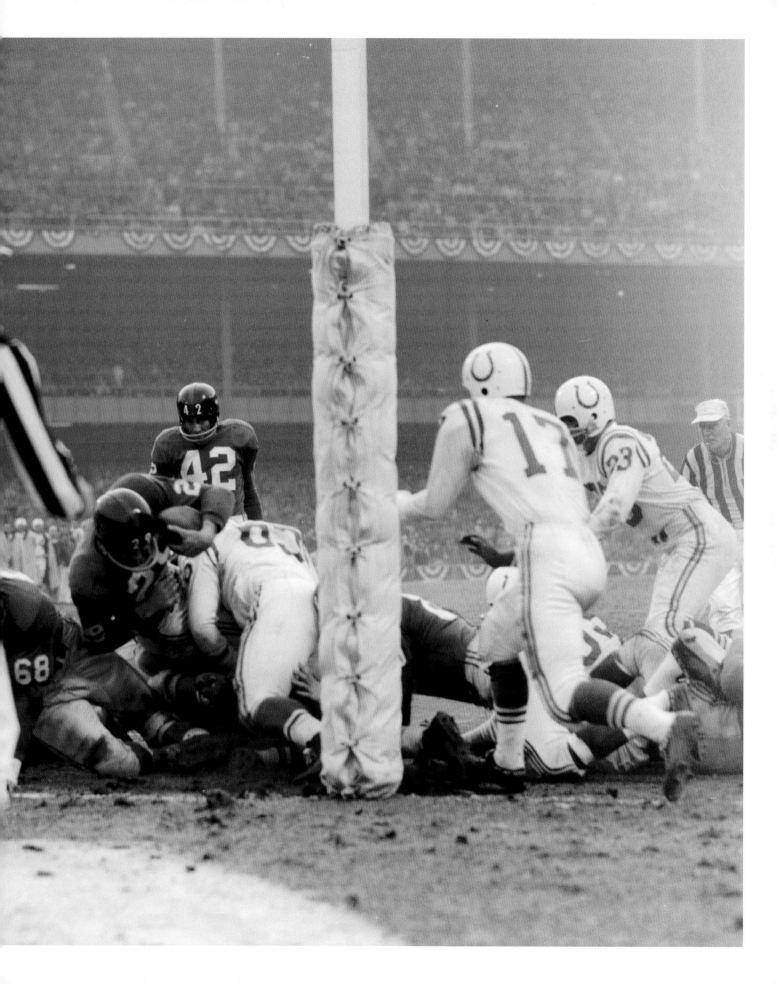

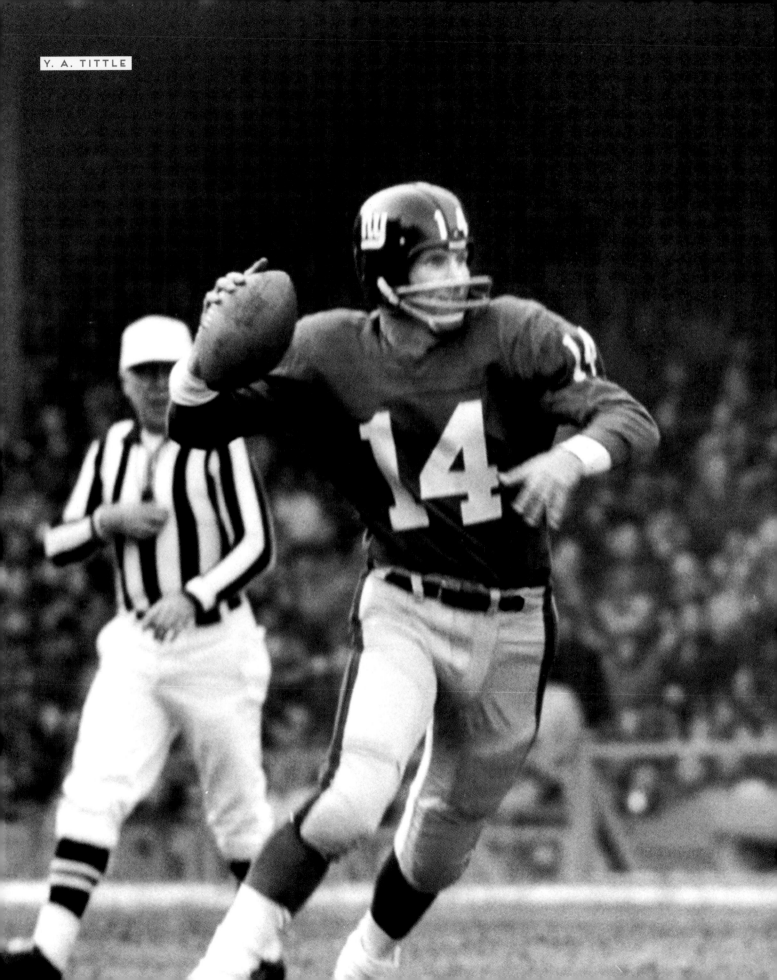

played in four different stadiums.

The Giants' prospects improved when they selected Phil Simms in the 1979 NFL Draft. He was a little-known quarterback. New York newspaper headlines read: "Phil Who?" During the next 14 seasons, Simms answered that question. Fans appreciated his talent, courage, and ability to perform in the clutch. His arrival signaled the start of the team's return to respectability.

PHIL SIMMS

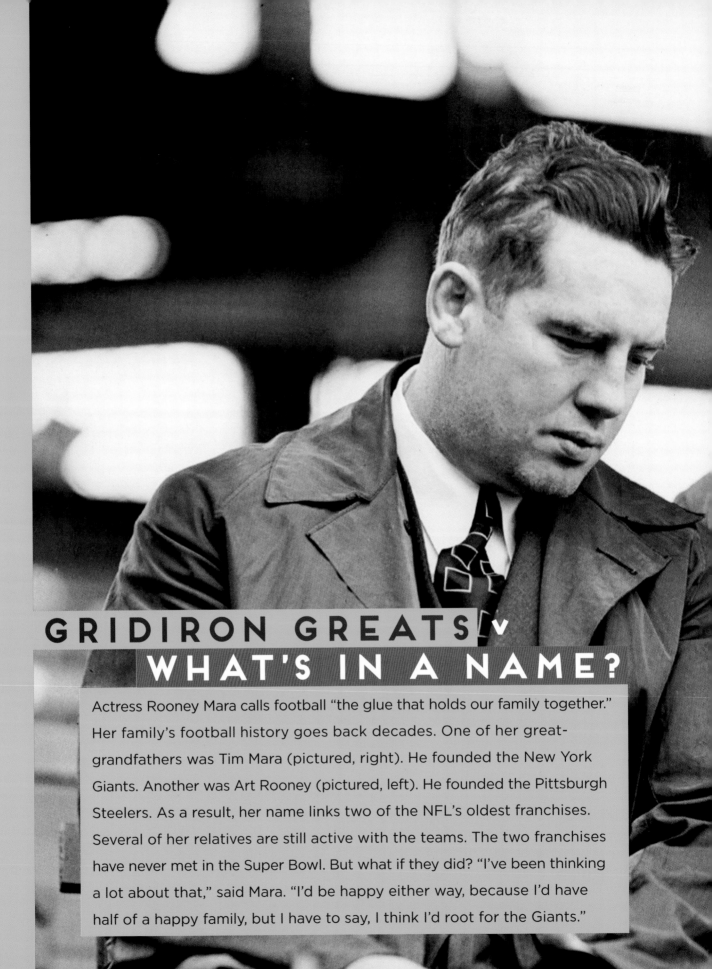

GRIDIRON GREATS
WHAT'S IN A NAME?

Actress Rooney Mara calls football "the glue that holds our family together." Her family's football history goes back decades. One of her great-grandfathers was Tim Mara (pictured, right). He founded the New York Giants. Another was Art Rooney (pictured, left). He founded the Pittsburgh Steelers. As a result, her name links two of the NFL's oldest franchises. Several of her relatives are still active with the teams. The two franchises have never met in the Super Bowl. But what if they did? "I've been thinking a lot about that," said Mara. "I'd be happy either way, because I'd have half of a happy family, but I have to say, I think I'd root for the Giants."

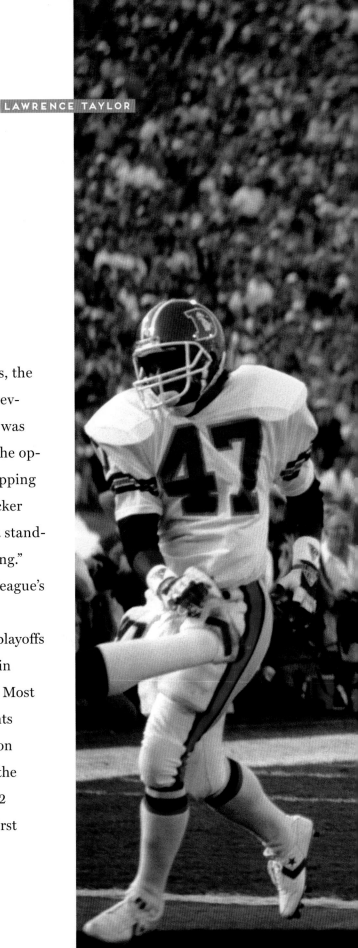

Two years after signing Simms, the team drafted linebacker Lawrence Taylor. Taylor revolutionized the position of outside linebacker. He was speedy and aggressive. He could anticipate what the opposing team was going to do. "He was actually stepping right with the snap of the ball," said fellow linebacker Brad Van Pelt. "While everybody else was still at a standstill, he was moving toward the ball—that's amazing." With Taylor's help, the Giants became one of the league's most exciting and feared teams.

Simms and Taylor propelled the Giants into the playoffs in 1981, 1984, and 1985. New York was even better in 1986. It finished 14–2. Taylor was named the NFL's Most Valuable Player (MVP). In the postseason, the Giants crushed the San Francisco 49ers and the Washington Redskins. They reached Super Bowl XXI opposite the Denver Broncos. Simms completed a remarkable 22 of 25 passes. The Giants won, 39–20. It was their first championship in 30 years.

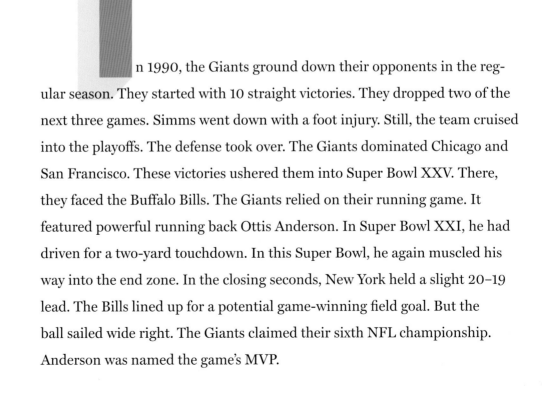

BEASTS OF THE EAST

In 1990, the Giants ground down their opponents in the regular season. They started with 10 straight victories. They dropped two of the next three games. Simms went down with a foot injury. Still, the team cruised into the playoffs. The defense took over. The Giants dominated Chicago and San Francisco. These victories ushered them into Super Bowl XXV. There, they faced the Buffalo Bills. The Giants relied on their running game. It featured powerful running back Ottis Anderson. In Super Bowl XXI, he had driven for a two-yard touchdown. In this Super Bowl, he again muscled his way into the end zone. In the closing seconds, New York held a slight 20–19 lead. The Bills lined up for a potential game-winning field goal. But the ball sailed wide right. The Giants claimed their sixth NFL championship. Anderson was named the game's MVP.

JEREMY SHOCKEY

Simms and Taylor retired after the 1993 season. Another golden era had ended in the Big Apple. In 1997, the Giants hired offensive specialist Jim Fassel as head coach. The team started slowly that year. Fans booed. Still, Fassel refused to make drastic changes. "That little red panic button is always there if you want to reach up and push it," he said. "But I would have lost [the players] right then if I started to make wholesale changes.... Everything I'd told them about being consistent and staying the course would have gone out the window." Boos soon turned to cheers. Fassel's new offensive system began to click. The team finished 10–5–1. In just one year, New York leaped from last to first in the National Football Conference (NFC) East Division.

In 2000, the Giants were ready for another championship run. Quarterback Kerry Collins led the team to 12 wins. Elusive running back Tiki Barber rushed for more than 1,000 yards. Defensive end Michael Strahan overpowered opponents. The Giants added two more wins in the playoffs. They met the Baltimore Ravens in Super Bowl XXXV. Unfortunately, the Ravens' defense shut them down. New York committed five turnovers. It lost, 34–7. "We didn't play well," said tackle Lomas Brown. "I'm just really disappointed to play this big of a game and not play well."

In 2002, the Giants drafted tight end Jeremy Shockey. He was an instant star. The rookie led all NFL tight ends in receptions and receiving yards. With a fiery personality, he was also the league's trash-talking leader. Shockey could catch passes and carry defenders on his back for big gains. This forced opponents to double-team him. His performance helped the Giants finish 10–6. They headed back to the playoffs. But their season ended in the Wild Card when they squandered a 24-point lead over the 49ers. The Giants lost, 39–38. The league admitted that the referees blew a call at the end of the game. It would have given New York the chance to kick a potential game-winning field goal.

TIKI BARBER

THE "OTHER" MANNING TAKES OVER

In 2004, the Giants acquired quarterback Eli Manning. He had been the top pick in the Draft. The San Diego Chargers selected him. But he refused to play for them. He went to the Giants in a trade. Manning made a lot of mistakes as a rookie. But nearly everyone believed he had a special talent that would eventually emerge. Manning's father, Archie, and older brother Peyton were star NFL quarterbacks. Eli lived up to this belief. He led the Giants to the playoffs in 2005. They lost the Wild Card. The first game of 2006 was dubbed the "Manning Bowl." Eli's Giants faced Peyton's Indianapolis Colts. It was the first NFL game with brothers quarterbacking

NEW YORK GIANTS

GRIDIRON GREATS ⌄
"LOOK, MA! ONE HAND!"

In November 2014, the Giants faced the Dallas Cowboys. Early in the second quarter, Eli Manning threw a long pass. The ball looked too high. Odell Beckham Jr. launched himself upward. He fully extended his right arm behind his head. Somehow, he plucked the ball from the air with his right hand. He held onto it as he fell into the end zone. "That may be the greatest catch I've ever seen," said a TV announcer. The Giants lost the game. But Beckham went on to record one of the greatest rookie seasons of all time. In just 12 games, he caught 91 receptions for 1,305 yards and 12 touchdowns.

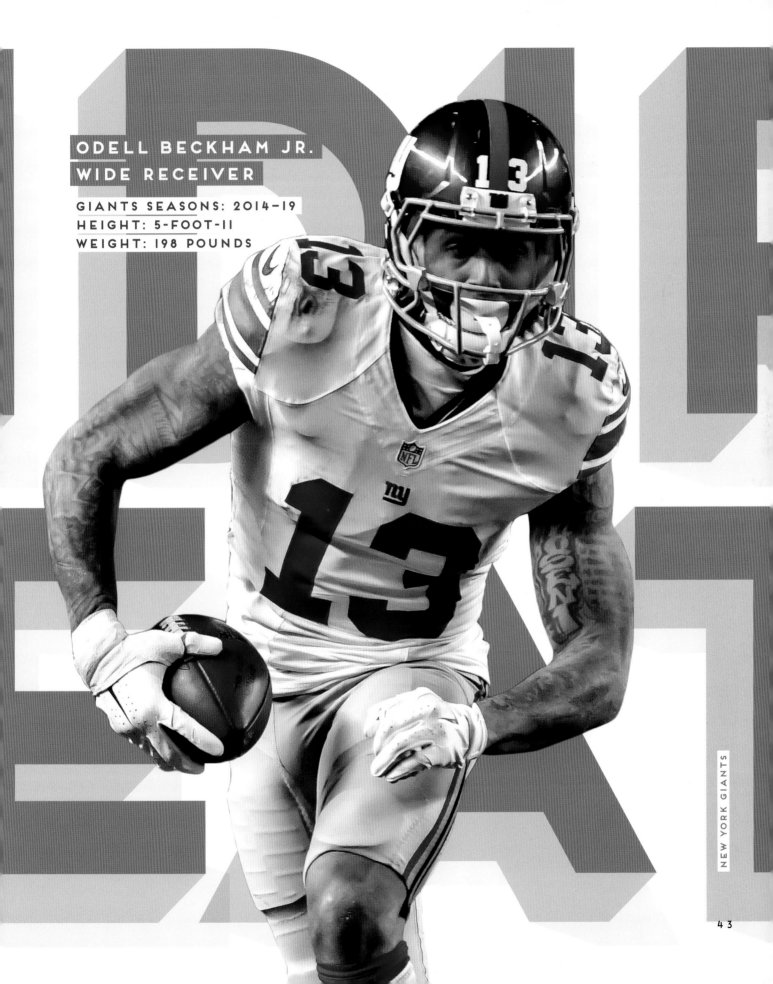

ODELL BECKHAM JR.
WIDE RECEIVER

GIANTS SEASONS: 2014-19
HEIGHT: 5-FOOT-11
WEIGHT: 198 POUNDS

NEW YORK GIANTS

43

opposing teams. Indianapolis won, 26–21. But Eli led the Giants to the postseason again.

After a slow start, the Giants finished 10–6 in 2007. They claimed a Wild Card berth. In three road games, Manning displayed a new confidence. The Giants won all of the games. They headed to the Super Bowl. With the aid of Tyree's "Helmet Catch," New York handed the Patriots a surprising defeat. Some experts thought that title had been a fluke. The 2008 Giants proved they were the real deal. They won 12 games. But they met a red-hot Philadelphia Eagles team in the playoffs. The Eagles beat New York, 23–11.

Manning was entering his prime years. The Giants wanted to make sure he had plenty of reliable targets. In 2009, they drafted wide receiver Hakeem Nicks. The following year, they added receiver Victor Cruz and tight end Jake Ballard. But the team missed the playoffs both seasons.

The following year began with a promising 6–2 start. Then New York lost four games in a row. It finished at 9–7. It squeaked into the playoffs. There, the Giants picked up steam. They defeated the Atlanta Falcons and the Packers. Then they eked out a 20–17 overtime win against San Francisco. They went to Super Bowl XLVI for a rematch with New England. Once again, a miraculous Manning pass—this time to Mario Manningham—sparked a late rally. New York grabbed the title with a 21–17 victory. It was the first team with fewer than 10 wins to become the Super Bowl champion.

The Giants went 9–7 again the following year. This time it wasn't good enough for the playoffs. Three losing seasons followed. Still, the team had exciting players. One

HAKEEM NICKS

MARIO MANNINGHAM

LINEBACKER OLIVIER VERNON

was wide receiver Odell Beckham Jr. He thrilled fans with his acrobatic catches. He was named Offensive Rookie of the Year in 2014. The Giants rebounded in 2016 with 11 wins. They moved back into the playoffs. But they gave up a season-high 38 points to Green Bay in the Wild Card. The next year, the Giants managed just a 3–13 mark. They finished the 2018 season at 5–11.

The New York Giants have four Super Bowl titles. They have another four NFL crowns from the pre-Super Bowl era. With this history, the Giants are among the league's most successful franchises. Almost a century ago, Tim Mara had no way of knowing how much of a return his $500 investment would generate. The team's founding father would certainly be proud of the way the Giants have represented the nation's largest city.

NFL CHAMPIONSHIPS

1927, 1934, 1938, 1956, 1986, 1990, 2007, 2011

WEBSITES

NEW YORK GIANTS

https://www.giants.com/

NFL: NEW YORK GIANTS TEAM PAGE

http://www.nfl.com/teams/newyorkgiants/profile?team=NYG

NEW YORK GIANTS

INDEX

WIDE RECEIVER AMANI TOOMER